C.S

MURDER S

John Townsend

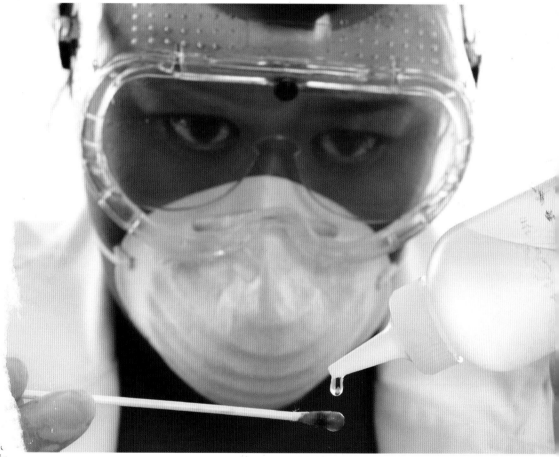

CLASH

by ticktock

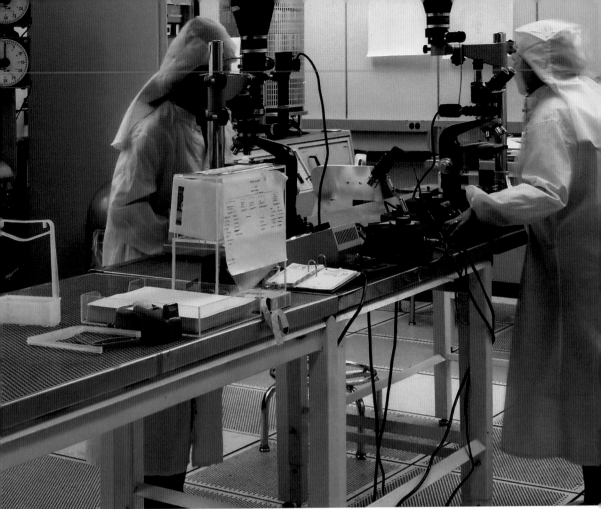

Copyright © ticktock Entertainment Ltd 2008

First published in Great Britain in 2008 by ticktock Media Ltd,
2 Orchard Business Centre, North Farm Road, Tunbridge Wells, Kent, TN2 3XF

ticktock project editor: Ruth Owen
ticktock project designer: Sara Greasley
ticktock picture researcher: Lizzie Knowles

**With thanks to series editors Honor Head and Jean Coppendale,
and consultant John Cassella, Principal Lecturer in Forensic Science, Staffordshire University, UK**

Thank you to Lorraine Petersen and the members of nasen

ISBN 978 1 84696 712 2 pbk

Printed in China

A CIP catalogue record for this book is available from the British Library.
No part of this publication may be reproduced, copied, stored in a retrieval system or transmitted in any form or
by any means electronic, mechanical, photocopying, recording or otherwise without prior written permission of
the copyright owner.

Picture credits (t=top; b=bottom; c=centre; l=left; r=right):
Peter Arnold, Inc./ Alamy: 21. Denis Closon/ Rex Features: 16. Eye of Science/ Science Photo Library: 22, 25t, 25bl.
Mauro Fermariello/ Science Photo Library: 5, 8, 14b. Steve Gschmeissner/ Science Photo Library: 18, 19. istock: 4tr,
20l, 23b, 24b, 28r, 24br. Jupiter Images/ Goodshoot: 27t. Mikael Karlsson/ Alamy: 14t. Richard Levine/ Alamy: 6b.
Peter Menzel/ Science Photo Library: 9. David Parker/ Science Photo Library: 11. Photolibrary/ fstop: 26/27. Philippe
Psaila/ Science Photo Library: 24. David Scharf/ Science Photo Library: 7 all. Shutterstock: OFC, 1, 2, 4tl, 6t, 10,
12/13, 16 inset, 17 all, 28l, 29, 31c. Superstock: 15, 23t. Andrew Syred/ Science Photo Library: 25br.

Every effort has been made to trace copyright holders, and we apologise in advance for any omissions. We would be
pleased to insert the appropriate acknowledgments in any subsequent edition of this publication.

Contents

CHAPTER 1

IT'S MURDER!

The police find a dead body in a room.

The victim was shot!

The police talk to the victim's family, friends and neighbours, and also to any witnesses.

Suspect A

Suspect B

The police arrest two people. Both suspects say they know each other but they don't know the victim.

The police must find evidence to prove if they are telling the truth or not.

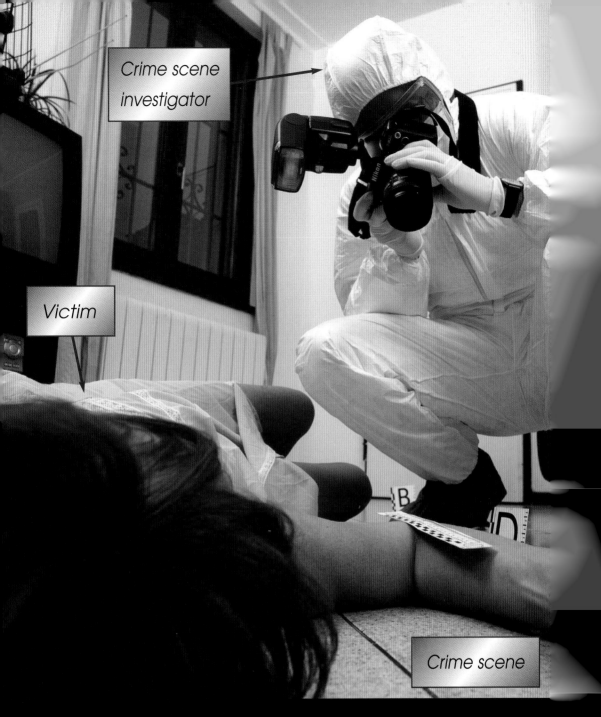

Crime scene investigator

Victim

Crime scene

Crime scene investigators (CSIs) look for evidence at the crime scene. They look for things such as fingerprints and hairs.

This is called trace evidence.

CHAPTER 2

AT THE CRIME LAB

The crime scene investigators take the trace evidence to the crime lab.

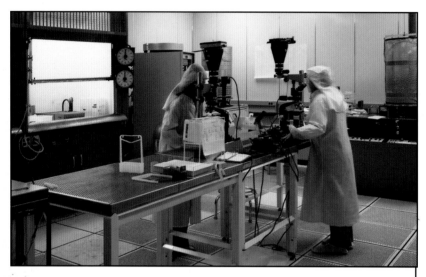

Powerful microscopes help the crime lab technicians look at tiny bits of evidence.

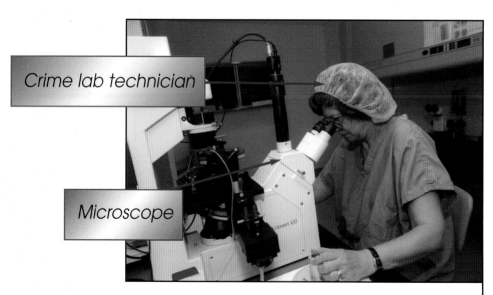

Crime lab technician

Microscope

A crime lab technician looks at dust from the crime scene.

When two things touch, tiny particles such as dust get moved from one object to another.

Dust from Suspect A

Dust on crime scene floor

Dust from Suspect B

Dust from one object is matched to dust on another. This proves if two objects have touched each other.

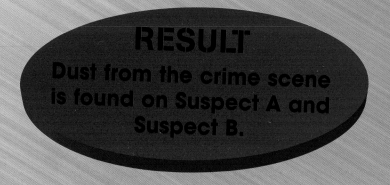

RESULT
Dust from the crime scene is found on Suspect A and Suspect B.

CHAPTER 3

BLOOD TRACES

Clothes from both suspects are sent to the crime lab.

A crime lab technician examines Suspect B's clothes. She is looking for traces of the victim's blood.

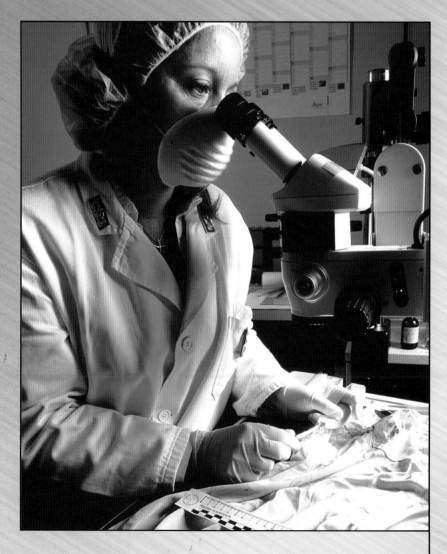

There are stains on the clothes. Is it blood?

Suspect A's clothes are examined and tested, too.

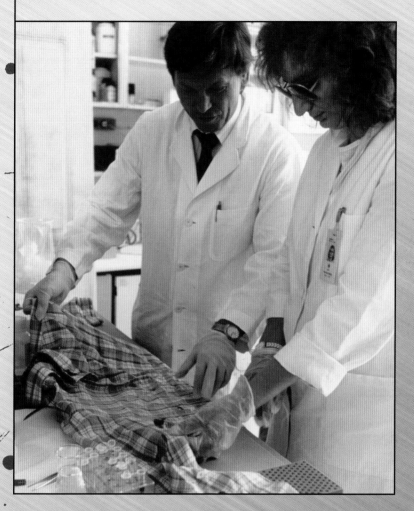

Just one spot of the victim's blood means the suspect was at the crime scene.

RESULT
Both suspects have blood on their clothes. But whose blood is it?

So where did the blood on the suspects come from?

DNA tests can prove if the blood came from the victim.

Cells in our blood are unique. Just like our fingerprints. The cells contain unique information called DNA.

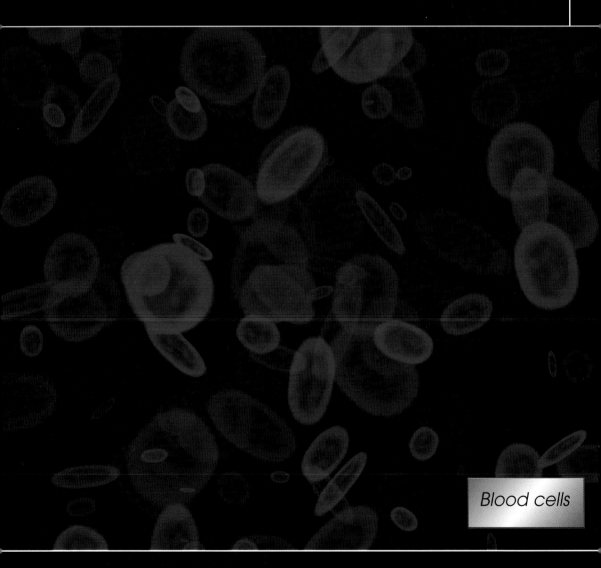

Blood cells

DNA tests are done on blood samples.
Special machines read the DNA.

They display the
information in a
pattern called
a profile.

DNA profile

A profile is made of the blood on the suspects' clothes.
Then a profile is made of the victim's blood.

If the profiles match, it means both blood samples are
from the same person.

RESULT
The blood on the clothes
of both the suspects is from
the victim.

CHAPTER 4 THE MURDER WEAPON

The police find a gun near the crime scene.

There is the smell of gunpowder.
There is gunshot discharge residue on the gun, too.

This means the gun has been fired recently.

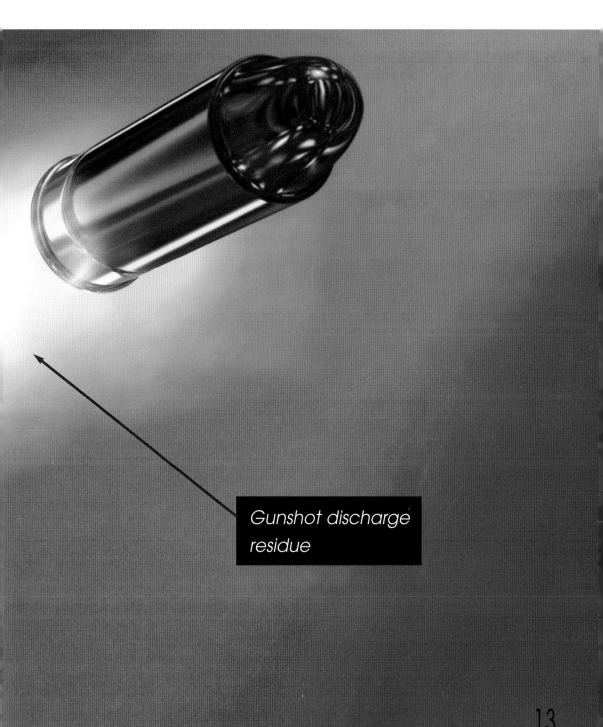

Gunshot discharge
residue

There are bullets in the dead body.

Tiny scratches on a bullet match marks inside a gun.

The gun from the crime scene is fired by a firearms expert. The bullets are compared to the bullets in the dead body.

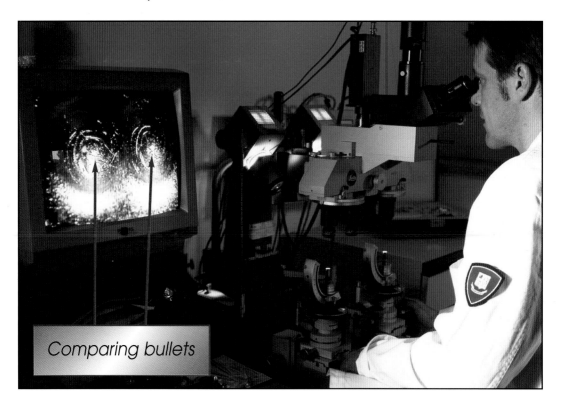

Comparing bullets

A crime lab technician uses a powerful microscope to compare the bullets.

The lab can prove if the gun fired the killing bullet. But it cannot prove who pulled the trigger.

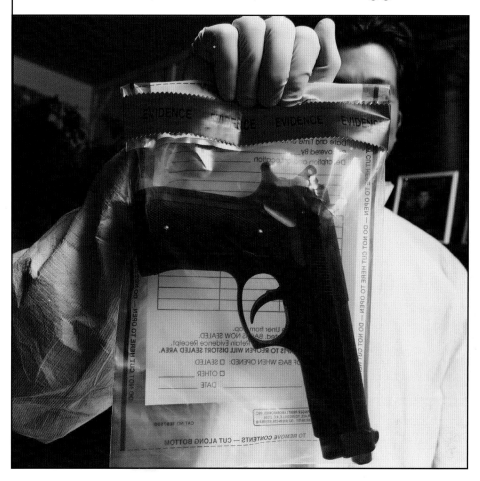

The lab might find gunpowder from the gun on a suspect's clothes. But it doesn't mean the suspect fired the gun. Anyone close to a firing gun can get traces on them.

RESULT
The gun killed the victim!
Traces from the gun are on
both suspects' clothes.

CHAPTER 5

TRACE EVIDENCE

A crime lab technician finds a fingerprint on the gun.

No two people have the same fingerprints.
Not even twins!

Whenever you touch something, you leave
a smear of grease, dust or sweat behind.

The fingerprint on the
gun is matched to prints
found at the crime scene.

Fingerprint on gun

Can you find a match to the print on the gun?

Bathroom

Victim

Suspect B

Suspect A

Front door

Bedroom

Kitchen knife

Coffee cup

Window

RESULT
**Suspect B's fingerprint
is on the gun.**

Next, a crime lab technician examines hairs on the clothes of the suspects.

Hairs are examined under a microscope.
The first job is to make sure it's human hair.
Then the technician finds out who the hairs belong to.

Hair

Skin

This is a close-up of dog hairs. Each hair has an outer layer of over-lapping scales.

The technician examines the hair root and measures its diameter and length. The technician also looks at the pattern of the scales and the colour of the hair.
DNA tests are also done on the hairs.

RESULT
Hairs on Suspect B's clothes came from the victim.

Hair

Skin

This is a close-up of human hairs.
The hairs look very different from dog hairs.

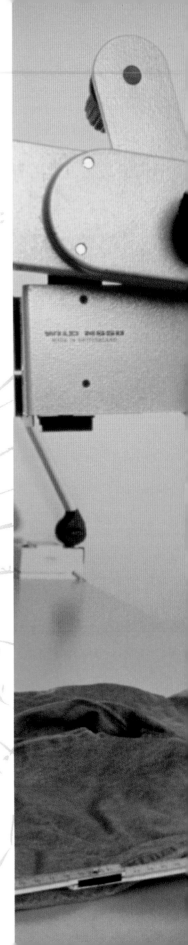

The killer got into the victim's house by breaking a window.

A crime lab technician finds glass on Suspect A's jeans.

No glass is exactly the same. A chemical test will show if the glass on the jeans is made exactly like the window glass.

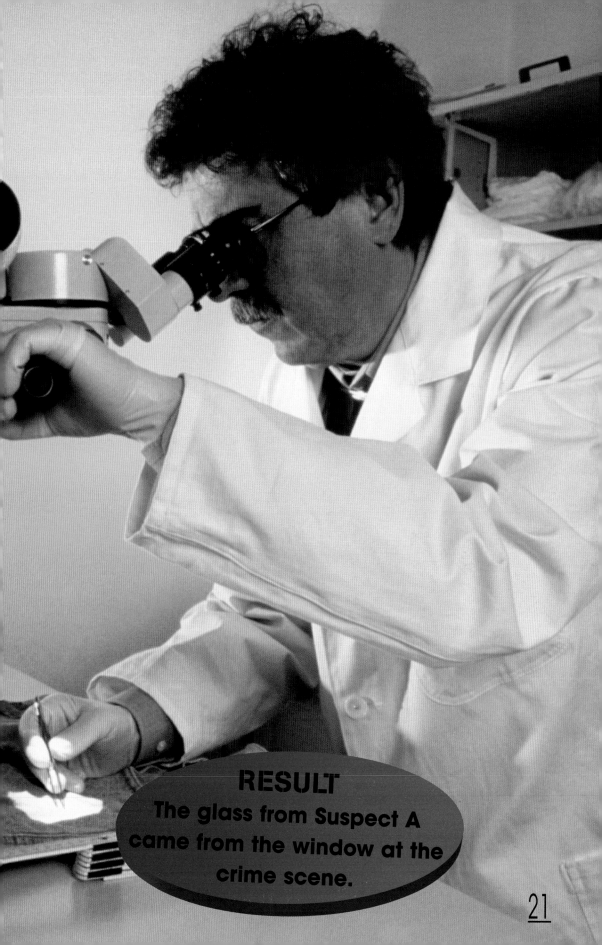

RESULT
The glass from Suspect A came from the window at the crime scene.

CHAPTER 6

A PUZZLE

A crime lab technician looks at the victim's socks under a microscope.

The socks are full of tiny specks. They are grains of pollen.

Grains of pollen

Tests show the pollen may have come from an ash tree.

But there are no ash trees near the crime scene.

The police visit the homes of the two suspects. There is an ash tree in Suspect B's garden.

The police search around the tree and find chewing gum under the tree.

The crime lab tests the chewing gum for saliva.

The saliva contains the victim's DNA!

RESULT
The victim had been to Suspect B's home. They knew each other.

Both suspects swear they have never been near the victim's house.

But then the CSIs find a shoeprint in the mud by the broken window.

They make a mould of the shoeprint and take it to the lab.

Mould of shoeprint

A technician matches the mould to the shoes of Suspect A and Suspect B.

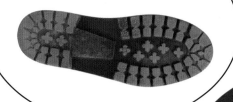

Suspect B's left shoe

RESULT
Suspect B's left shoe made the shoeprint.

Suspect B must be guilty!

But then the lab technician finds more trace evidence. Inside Suspect B's shoe are tiny fibres.

Fibres in shoe

Manmade fibre

Sheep's wool

The lab technician looks at the fibres under a microscope.

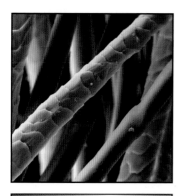

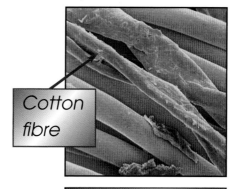

Cotton fibre

Suspect A's socks

Suspect B's socks

The fibres do not match Suspect B's socks. They match the socks of Suspect A!

RESULT
Suspect A wore
Suspect B's shoe to make
a false shoeprint

FINAL PROOF

Suspect A still says he never met the victim. The police look at a bite on his arm. He says it's a dog bite.

The police photograph the bite and send pictures to the crime lab. A lab technician has a theory.

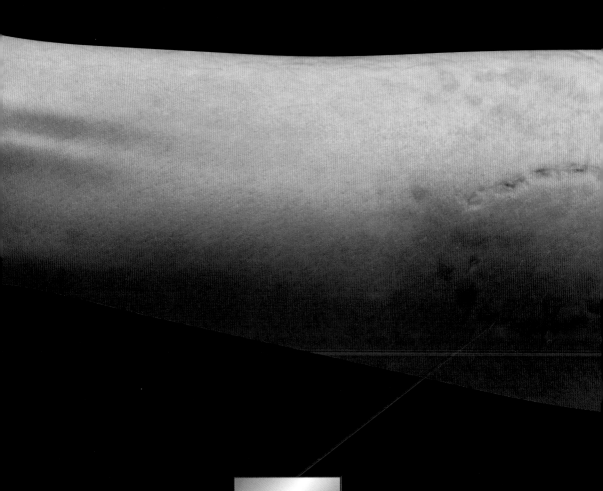

Bite mark

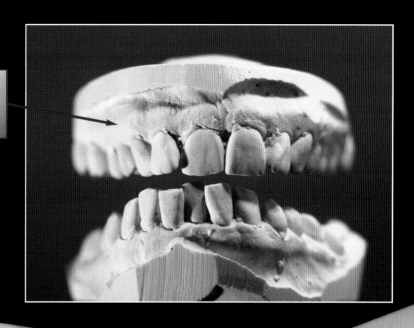

Mould of victim's teeth

The crime lab make a mould of the victim's teeth.
They scan this into a computer and make a 3-D image.
The victim's teeth match the bite on Suspect A's arm.

It is not a dog bite. The victim bit Suspect A!

THE CHARGE

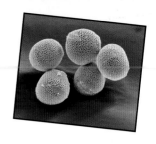

LAB REPORT: SUSPECT A

EVIDENCE	MATCH
Dust	✓
Victim's blood on clothes	✓
Gunshot discharge residue	✓
Fingerprint on gun	X
Victim's hair on clothes	X
Glass	✓
Pollen	X
Chewing gum	X
Shoeprint	X
Sock fibre	✓ in B's shoe
Bite from victim	✓

Statement:

I never knew the victim and was never at the crime scene. I've been framed!

G675-9048

Suspect A

Suspect A is charged with murder.

In court, Suspect A is found guilty of the murder.

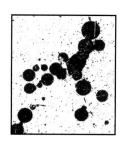

LAB REPORT: SUSPECT B

EVIDENCE	MATCH
Dust	✓
Victim's blood on clothes	✓
Gunshot discharge residue	✓
Fingerprint on gun	✓
Victim's hair on clothes	✓
Glass	X
Pollen	✓
Chewing gum	✓
Shoeprint	✓ planted
Sock fibre	X
Bite from victim	X

Statement:
I found the body and tried to help. I saw the gun and picked it up. I was scared to say I knew her.

G675-9049

Suspect B

Suspect B was a witness to the crime.

She got trace evidence on her when she found the body.

CASE SOLVED!

NEED TO KNOW WORDS

3-D image An image on a computer screen, or in a book, that looks solid, not flat. 3-D is short for three-dimensional.

crime lab A laboratory with equipment that is used for scientific tests and experiments. The tests are carried out on crime scene evidence.

crime scene Any place where a crime has happened.

deny To refuse to admit the truth or accept the truth.

diameter The width of a circle.

DNA The special code in the centre (or nucleus) of each person's cells. DNA makes each person unique.

evidence Facts and signs that can show what happened during a crime.

fibre A tiny thread.

firearms expert A scientist who tests guns and bullets.

framed When an innocent person is made to look as if they are guilty.

guilty When someone has done something wrong, such as committing a crime.

innocent Free from guilt or blame.

pollen Tiny grains that look like dust. Pollen is made by flowers and trees.

saliva The spit that is made in your mouth.

suspect A person who the police think has committed a crime.

trace A very small mark, sign or substance that is left behind.

unique The only one of its kind.

victim A person who is hurt or killed.

witness Someone who saw a crime being committed or who has information about a crime.

LIFE IN THE LAB

There are many different jobs to be done in the crime lab.

- **Prints expert**
Crime lab technicians examine and compare fingerprints, shoeprints and tyre marks. They match crime scene fingerprints with fingerprints of known criminals. They use a database which holds millions of fingerprint records.

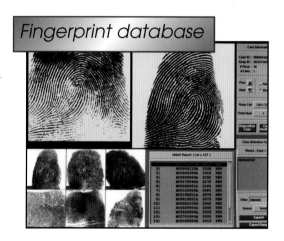

Fingerprint database

- **Drugs and poisons expert**
Crime lab technicians analyse poisons, drugs and alcohol. If a murder victim has been poisoned, they test samples of the victim's hair, blood and skin.

- **Firearms expert**
Firearms experts identify and test guns. They also identify and compare bullets. A firearms expert can work out the distance of a gun from a gunshot victim.

- **Documents expert**
Technicians look for changes to important papers or letters. They also look for papers or letters that have been forged. They compare samples of handwriting. They can even reconstruct documents that have been destroyed.

CRIME ONLINE

Websites

www.fbi.gov/kids/6th12th/6th12th.htm
How the FBI investigates crimes

www.howstuffworks.com/csi5.htm
All about the world of crime scene investigation

library.thinkquest.org/04oct/00206/tte_every_criminal_leaves_a _trace.htm "Let evidence reveal the truth"

www.sciencenewsforkids.org/articles/20041215/wordfind.asp
A science site that includes a crime lab wordsearch

INDEX